D0816642

My Skin Is Gray and Wrinkly

by Joyce Markovics

Consultants:
Christopher Kuhar, PhD
Executive Director
Cleveland Metroparks Zoo
Cleveland, Ohio

Kimberly Brenneman, PhD
National Institute for Early Education Research
Rutgers University
New Brunswick, New Jersey

BEARPORT PUBLISHING

New York, New York

Credits

Cover, © Louise Murray/Alamy; 4–5, © Scott Camazine/Alamy; 6–7, © Steve Bloom Images/Alamy; 8–9, © Shantell/iStockphoto; 10–11, © Purestock/Thinkstock; 12–13, © Fuse/Thinkstock; 14–15, © Ingo Arndt/naturepl.com; 16–17, © Lukas Blazek/Dreamstime.com; 18–19, © Paul Souders/Corbis; 20–21, © Paul Souders/Corbis; 22, © RGB Ventures LLC dba SuperStock/Alamy; 23, © ericlefrancais/Shutterstock; 24, © iStock/Thinkstock.

Publisher: Kenn Goin
Senior Editor: Joyce Tavolacci
Creative Director: Spencer Brinker
Design: Debrah Kaiser
Photo Researcher: Michael Win

Library of Congress Cataloging-in-Publication Data

Markovics, Joyce L.
   My skin is gray and wrinkly / by Joyce Markovics ; consultant: Christopher Kuhar, PhD, Executive Director Cleveland Metroparks Zoo, Cleveland, Ohio.
      pages cm. — (Zoo clues)
   Includes bibliographical references and index.
   ISBN-13: 978-1-62724-109-0 (library binding)
   ISBN-10: 1-62724-109-4 (library binding)
   1. Walrus—Juvenile literature. I. Title.
   QL737.P62M28 2014
   599.79'9—dc23

                        2013035385

For more information, write to Bearport Publishing Company, Inc., 45 West 21st Street, Suite 3B, New York, New York 10010. Printed in the United States of America.

10 9 8 7 6 5 4 3 2 1

Contents

What Am I?

Look at my front teeth.

They are large
and long.

5

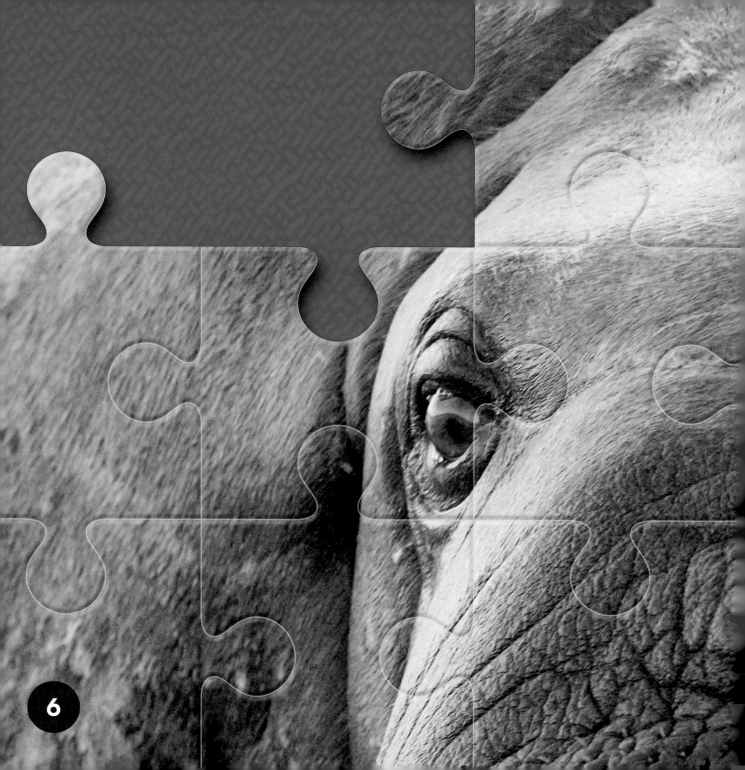

My eyes are
small and brown.

7

I have four,
flat flippers.

Each flipper has five toes.

My ears are
tiny holes.

I have two,
large nostrils.

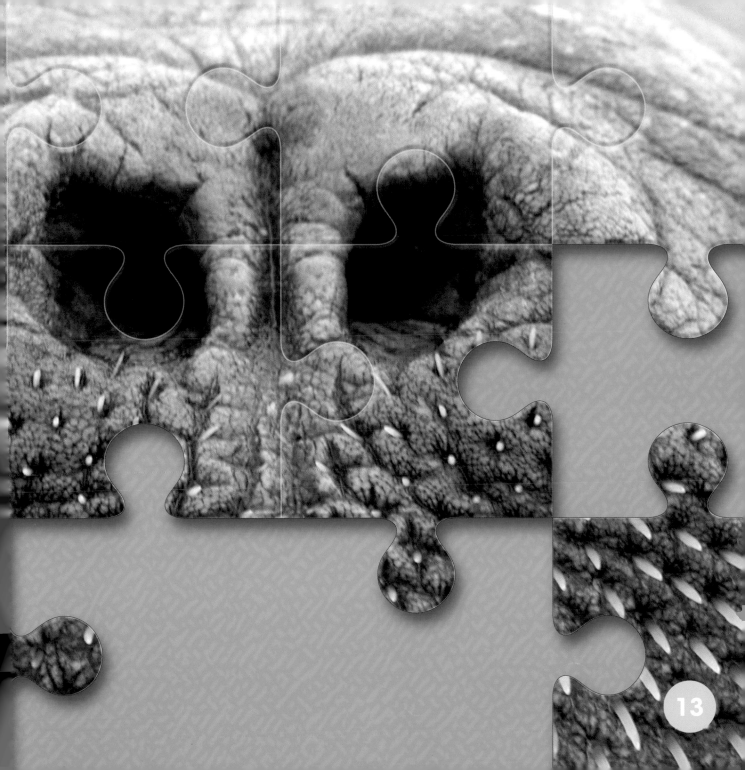

13

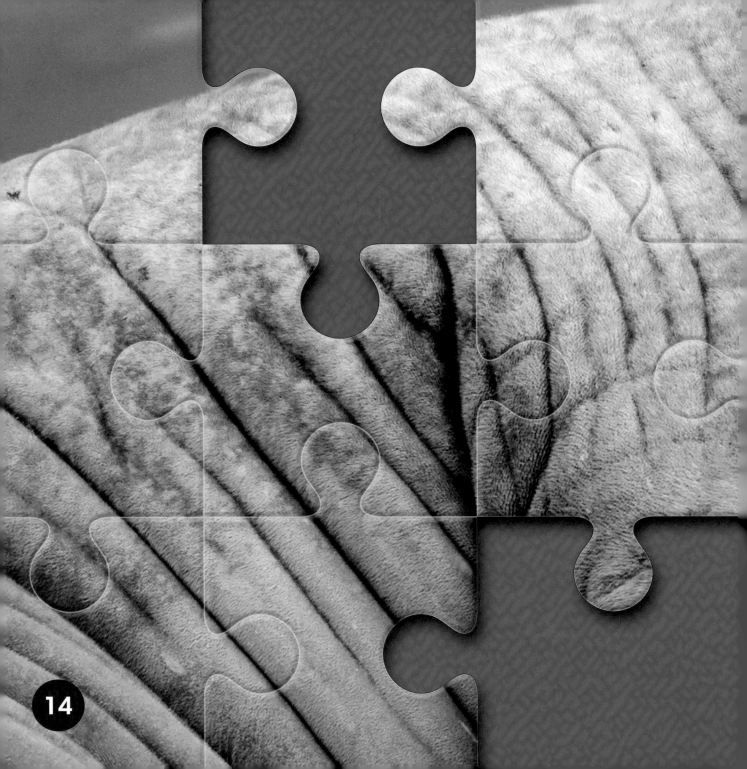

My skin is gray
and wrinkly.

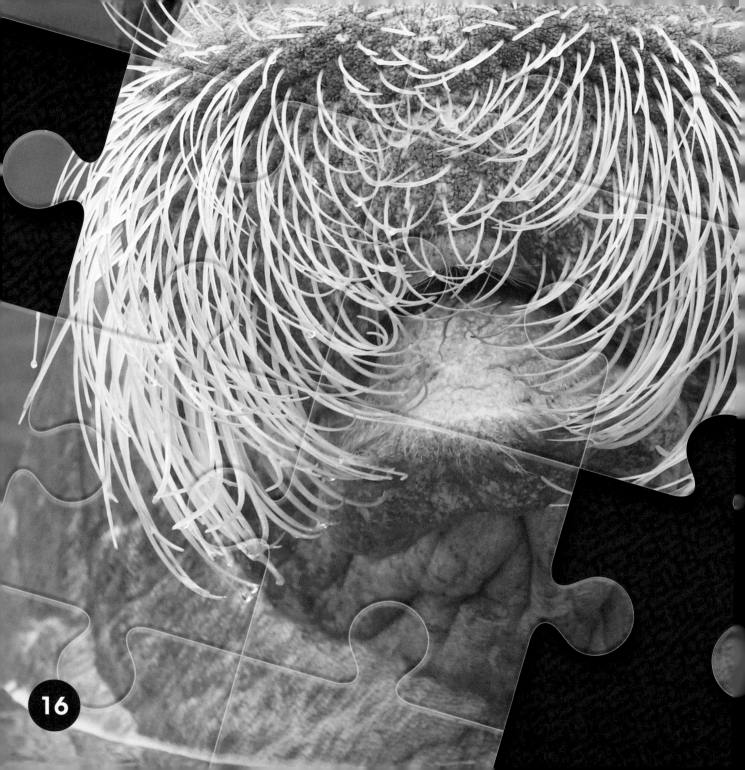

16

I have hundreds
of whiskers.

What am I?

Let's find out!

I am a walrus!

21

Animal Facts

Walruses are mammals. Like almost all mammals, they give birth to live young. The babies drink milk from their mothers. Mammals also have hair or fur on their skin.

More Walrus Facts

Food:	Clams, crabs, snails, and worms
Size:	7 to 11.5 feet (2 to 3.5 m) long
Weight:	Up to 3,000 pounds (1,361 kg)
Life Span:	Up to 40 years
Cool Fact:	A walrus's tusks can grow as long as 3 feet (0.9 m)!

Adult Walrus Size

Where Do I Live?

Walruses live in oceans in the far north. They are able to live in very cold water because they have a thick layer of fat called blubber.

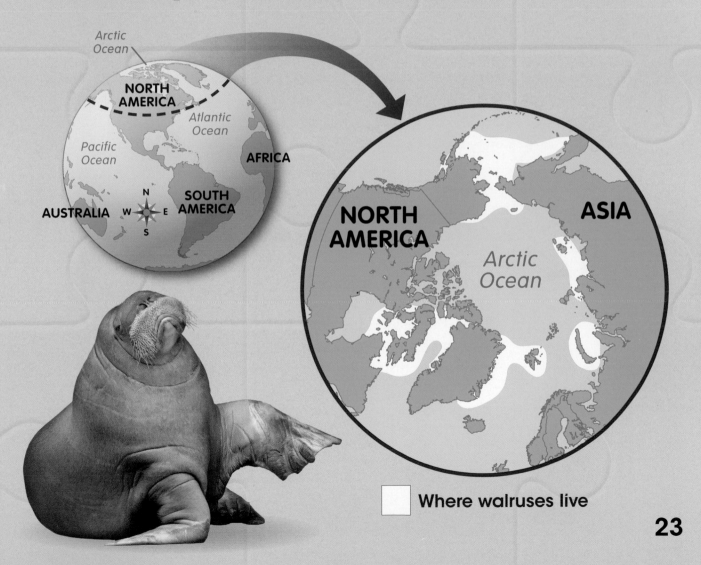

Where walruses live

Index

Read More

Miller, Sara Swan. *Walruses of the Arctic (Brrr! Polar Animals).* New York: PowerKids Press (2009).

Sexton, Colleen A. *Walruses (Blastoff! Readers: Oceans Alive).* Minneapolis, MN: Bellwether Media (2008).

Learn More Online

To learn more about walruses, visit
www.bearportpublishing.com/ZooClues

About the Author

Joyce Markovics lives along the Hudson River in Tarrytown, New York. She enjoys spending time with furry, finned, and feathered creatures.